Nanobots to the Rescue

Happy House

About Wise & Wide

- A systematic 6-level English reading program based on Lexile® measures
- Diverse and interesting topics chosen from the elementary curriculums of Korea and English speaking western countries
- Well-written books in various forms including fiction stories, descriptive texts, and classics retold
- The informative but original fiction stories grab your interest, leading to the easy and clear understanding of the educational content.
- Improve thinking skills with solid after-reading activities at all levels of the series.

Wise & Wide is a 6-level English reading program that consists of 60 books and each level is systematically divided by Lexile® measures. The Lexile® Framework for Reading is the most popular reading measuring system in American formal education curriculums and many English programs. Over 20 out of 50 states in the U.S. mark Lexile® measures directly on students' final report cards and over 300 well-known publishers adopt and use Lexile® measures.

Experience many kinds of readings written by professional writers from the U.S. and England. They used interesting topics that were carefully chosen after analyzing elementary curriculums from around the world including Korea, the U.S., England, and Australia among many others. Comprehensive after-reading activities including graphic organizers, speaking tasks, and After-reading Tests are ready for you.

Levels in the series and their corresponding Lexile® measures

Level	Lexile® measures	U.S. Grade
Level 1	Below 200L	Pre K - K
Level 2	190L - 400L	Lower Grade 1
Level 3	350L - 530L	Upper Grade 1
Level 4	420L - 650L	Grade 2
Level 5	520L - 940L	Grade 3 - 4
Level 6	830L - 1070L	Grade 5 - 6

* Smart Readers: Wise & Wide level 1 is applicable to the preschool level in the U.S.

* The source of the relationship between Lexile® measures and U.S. school grades: CCSS(Common Core State Standards) FOR ENGLISH LANGUAGE ARTS, APPENDIX A (2012, which is used by 45 states in the U.S.)

Topic List

	Level 1	Level 2	Level 3	Level 4	Level 5	Level 6
Book 1	Science>Biology: The hibernation of animals Story	Science>Biology: Living and nonliving things Story	Science>Biology> Animals & the Environment: Sea otters Story	Environment> Living with nature: The diver & the persimmon tree Story	Science>Biology> Animal: Amazing animals of the Amazon Story	Science>Biology: Germs, transmitted diseases Story
Book 2	Literature> World classics: Aesop's fables Story	Literature> Traditional fairy tale: Old tales about stones Story	Social Studies> Economy: To run a business to make and save money Story	Science>Biology> Plants: Photosynthesis Story	Science>Earth science: Earth's layers, earthquakes, volcanoes, and earth's atmosphere Report	Mathematics> Sequence: The golden ratio & the Fibonacci sequence Story
Book 3	Science>Physics: How shadows are formed Story	Literature> World classics: Peter Pan Story	Science>Scientific technology: Nanobots Story	Literature>Myths: World's creation stories Story	Literature> Legend: The story of King Arthur Story	
Book 4	Literature> Traditional literature: The Talmud Story	Science>Biology> Animal: Polar bears Story	Science>Biology> Animal: Mountain gorillas Story	Social Studies> Cultural anthropology: Amazing ancient cultures of the world Story	Science> Earth science: Clouds and weather Story	
Book 5			Social Studies> Cultural anthropology: Astonishing festivals Report	Art>Music: Stories from two operas Story		
Book 6				Social Studies> People: Three great people who overcame hardships Story		
Book 7						
Book 8						
Book 9						
Book 10						

* 10 books in each level will be published.

How to Use This Book

•Before Reading

You can easily find the topic and what kind of story you are about to read.

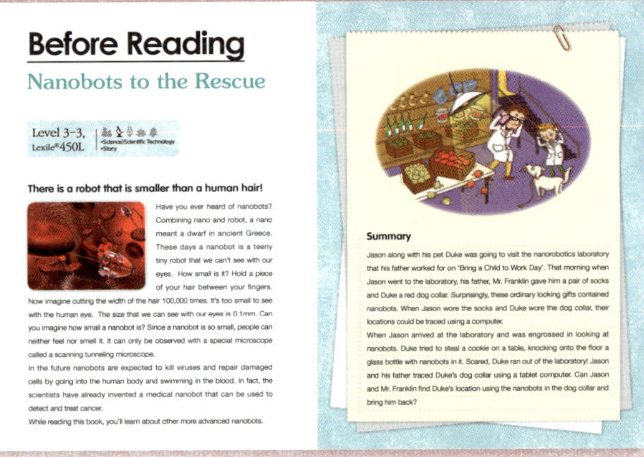

•The text

All the stories were written by professional writers from the U.S. and England, so you will read authentic and appropriate English sentences and expressions in every book in the series.

•Pop Quiz

Check out right away if you understand what you have just read by solving a pop quiz that checks your comprehension.

•Key Words

The key words and expressions on each page are listed for you to easily study them.

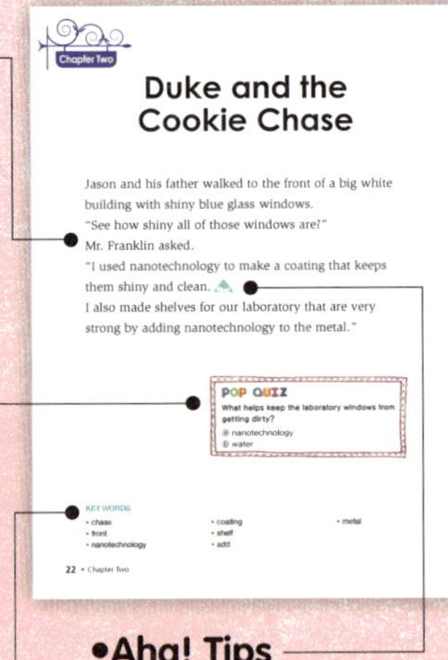

•Aha! Tips

Download free Korean explanations at *www.ihappyhouse.co.kr* for all of the sentences marked with "Aha!". These explain cultural, scientific, and economic knowledge or they deal with aspects of English such as grammatical structures or idiomatic expressions. There are lots of "Aha! Tips" to help you understand the text.

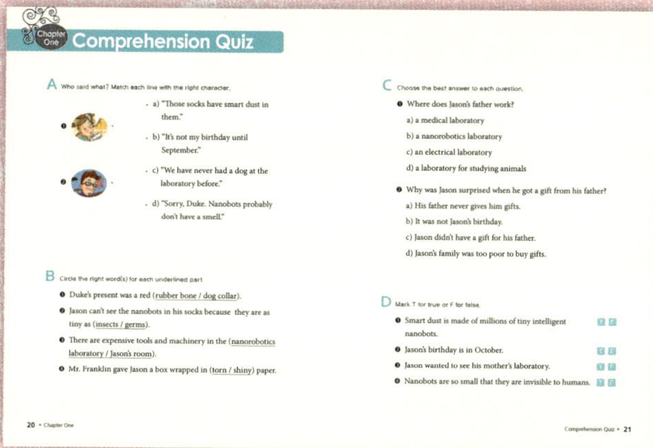

•Comprehension Quiz

After reading one chapter, solve various questions to find out if you fully understand the content.

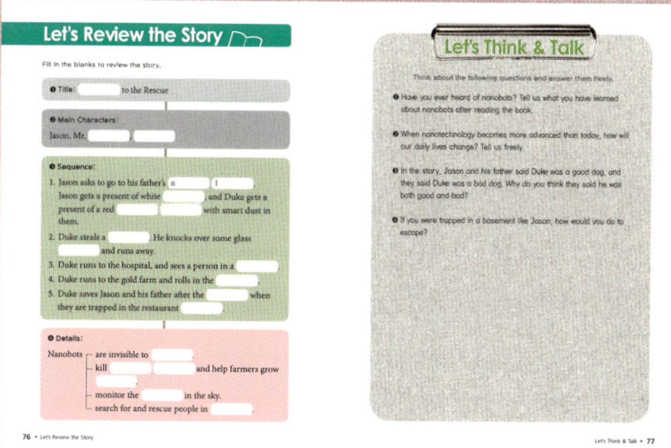

•Let's Review the Story /
•Let's Think & Talk

Fill in the blanks in the organizer to summarize the whole story. Express your own thinking and feelings about the story by answering the questions. You can build up logic and reasoning skills for your essay examinations in the future.

Appendix

Audio CD

In the CD audio book form, the texts are read vividly by American professional voice actors.

After-reading Test

Solve an additionally provided After-reading Test for each book.

The Korean translation, Answer Keys, a Word Quiz, a Word List, and Aha! Tips for each book

You can download them for free at *www.ihappyhouse.co.kr*

Before Reading

Nanobots to the Rescue

Level 3–3,
Lexile® 450L

•Science〉Scientific Technology
•Story

There is a robot that is smaller than a human hair!

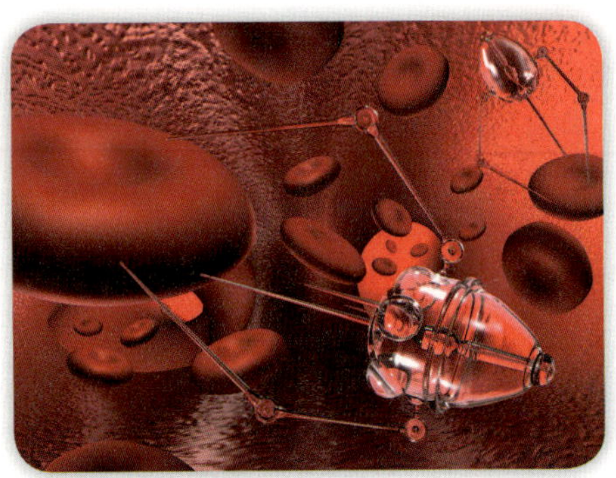

Have you ever heard of nanobots? Combining nano and robot, a nano meant a dwarf in ancient Greece. These days a nanobot is a teeny tiny robot that we can't see with our eyes. How small is it? Hold a piece of your hair between your fingers. Now imagine cutting the width of the hair 100,000 times. It's too small to see with the human eye. The size that we can see with our eyes is 0.1mm. Can you imagine how small a nanobot is? Since a nanobot is so small, people can neither feel nor smell it. It can only be observed with a special microscope called a scanning tunneling microscope.

In the future nanobots are expected to kill viruses and repair damaged cells by going into the human body and swimming in the blood. In fact, the scientists have already invented a medical nanobot that can be used to detect and treat cancer.

While reading this book, you'll learn about other more advanced nanobots.

Summary

Jason along with his pet Duke was going to visit the nanorobotics laboratory that his father worked for on 'Bring a Child to Work Day'. That morning when Jason went to the laboratory, his father, Mr. Franklin gave him a pair of socks and Duke a red dog collar. Surprisingly, these ordinary looking gifts contained nanobots. When Jason wore the socks and Duke wore the dog collar, their locations could be traced using a computer.

When Jason arrived at the laboratory and was engrossed in looking at nanobots. Duke tried to steal a cookie on a table, knocking onto the floor a glass bottle with nanobots in it. Scared, Duke ran out of the laboratory! Jason and his father traced Duke's dog collar using a tablet computer. Can Jason and Mr. Franklin find Duke's location using the nanobots in the dog collar and bring him back?

Contents

Nanobots to the Rescue

Nanobots to the Rescue

Nanobot Smart Dust

Jason Franklin circled a date on the family calendar with a red pen.

Jason showed his father the calendar at dinner.

"Dad, may I go to see your laboratory?"

Mr. Franklin looked at the date.

"June 14 is Bring a Child to Work Day. **Aha!** That will be a good time for you to visit my nanorobotics laboratory. You'll get to see the future of science."

Jason grinned.

"May Duke go, too?"

"I don't know if that's a good idea."

His father rubbed his chin.

"We have never had a dog at the laboratory before."

"Please, Dad?"

Jason did not want to beg, but it would be fun to have Duke go, too.

KEY WORDS

- nanobot
- dust
- circle a date on the calendar
- show
- may
- **go to see** (go-went-gone)
- **Bring a Child to Work Day** (bring-brought-brought)
- work
- nanorobotics laboratory
- grin
- rub one's chin
- beg

Mr. Franklin looked at the dog and shook his head.

"Nanobots are very sensitive technology.

We use expensive tools and machinery to make them."

Duke barked and wagged his tail.

"See, Dad? Duke wants to go.

He'll be a smart Labrador in the lab."

Jason's father laughed.

"Okay, son. Duke may go,

but he needs to behave

himself."

"Duke is a good dog.

He will behave. Won't you,

Duke?"

Duke sat down to show what a

good dog he could be.

KEY WORDS

- **shake one's head** (shake-shook-shaken)
- **sensitive**
- **technology**
- **tool**
- **machinery**
- **bark**
- **wag**
- **Labrador**
- **behave oneself**
- **train**
- **walk on a leash**
- **stay**
- **get into trouble** (get-got-gotten)
- **arrive**
- **wake up** (wake-woke-woken)
- **wrapped**
- **shiny**
- **wear** (wear-wore-worn)

Jason worked hard training Duke to walk on a leash, sit, and stay.

He did not want Duke to get into trouble.

Finally, June 14 arrived.

Mr. Franklin woke Jason up early.

He gave Jason a box wrapped in shiny paper.

"What is this?" Jason asked.

"It's not my birthday until September."

"It's something special.

I want you to wear them today."

Jason loved getting presents.

This was starting out to be a very special day.

He grinned and unwrapped the package.

It was a pair of socks—a pair of white socks.

A pair of ordinary, everyday white socks.

Jason swallowed hard to hide his disappointment.

"Um, thank you, Dad." His father laughed.

"Those are not regular socks. They are special.

Those socks have smart dust in them."

KEY WORDS

- start out
- unwrap (↔ wrap)
- package
- a pair of socks
- ordinary
- swallow hard
- hide one's disappointment (hide-hid-hidden)
- regular

"What is smart dust?"

Jason wrinkled his nose as if he might sneeze.

"Smart dust is made of millions of tiny intelligent nanobots. They keep your feet dry and cool on hot days. They help cuts heal.

They can also track where you go.

If you get lost, I can find you by using my computer to contact the nanobots in your socks."

KEY WORDS

- wrinkle
- as if
- sneeze
- be made of
- millions of
- intelligent
- cut
- heal
- track
- get lost (lose-lost-lost)
- contact

"Will they make me run faster?"

Mr. Franklin laughed.

"I don't think so, son."

Jason peered at his new socks.

He turned them over.

"I don't see anything."

"Nanobots are very small. They are as tiny as germs.

They are so small that they are invisible to humans.

We can only see them with a scanning tunneling

microscope. **Aha!**

But there can be one million nanobots in one millimeter."

"That's small!" Jason rubbed his fingers on his new socks.

"You can't feel them either."

KEY WORDS

- peer at
- turn over
- as tiny as
- germ
- invisible
- scanning tunneling microscope

- millimeter $(1mm = \frac{1}{1000}m)$
- put on (put-put-put)
- sniff
- hand
- get better
- by the minute

Jason put on the socks.

"You're right! I can't feel them at all."

Duke sniffed Jason's feet and smelled the socks.

"Sorry, Duke. Nanobots probably don't have a smell,"
Jason said.

"I have something special for Duke, too."

Jason's father took another wrapped present out of his
pocket.

He let Duke sniff the present. He handed it to Jason.

"Would you like to open the present for Duke?"

This day was getting better by the minute.

Jason tore the paper off the package.

It was a red dog collar — a plain, ordinary, everyday red dog collar.

"I thought it would be a rope toy or a rubber bone."

"This dog collar is better than a treat.

It has nanobots in it, too."

"What do the nanobots in his collar do?"

"Like your socks, they will tell us where Duke goes.

That way, he can't get lost at the laboratory."

"Duke is a good dog. He will stay with me all day."

Jason patted his dog on the head.

"Isn't that right, Duke?"

Duke barked and wagged his tail.

"See, Dad? Nothing will go wrong."

KEY WORDS

- **tear off** (tear-tore-torn)
- **dog collar**
- **plain**
- **rubber bone**
- **treat**
- **that way**
- **pat**
- **go wrong**

Chapter One

Comprehension Quiz

A Who said what? Match each line with the right character.

❶

❷

a) "Those socks have smart dust in them."

b) "It's not my birthday until September."

c) "We have never had a dog at the laboratory before."

d) "Sorry, Duke. Nanobots probably don't have a smell."

B Circle the right word(s) for each underlined part.

❶ Duke's present was a red (<u>rubber bone</u> / <u>dog collar</u>).

❷ Jason can't see the nanobots in his socks because they are as tiny as (<u>insects</u> / <u>germs</u>).

❸ There are expensive tools and machinery in the (<u>nanorobotics laboratory</u> / <u>Jason's room</u>).

❹ Mr. Franklin gave Jason a box wrapped in (<u>torn</u> / <u>shiny</u>) paper.

  Choose the best answer to each question.

❶ Where does Jason's father work?

    a) a medical laboratory

    b) a nanorobotics laboratory

    c) an electrical laboratory

    d) a laboratory for studying animals

❷ Why was Jason surprised when he got a gift from his father?

    a) His father never gives him gifts.

    b) It was not Jason's birthday.

    c) Jason didn't have a gift for his father.

    d) Jason's family was too poor to buy gifts.

D Mark T for true or F for false.

❶ Smart dust is made of millions of tiny intelligent nanobots.   T F

❷ Jason's birthday is in October.   T F

❸ Jason wanted to see his mother's laboratory.   T F

❹ Nanobots are so small that they are invisible to humans.   T F

Duke and the Cookie Chase

Jason and his father walked to the front of a big white building with shiny blue glass windows.

"See how shiny all of those windows are?"

Mr. Franklin asked.

"I used nanotechnology to make a coating that keeps them shiny and clean. **Aha!**

I also made shelves for our laboratory that are very strong by adding nanotechnology to the metal."

POP QUIZ

What helps keep the laboratory windows from getting dirty?

ⓐ nanotechnology

ⓑ water

KEY WORDS

- chase
- front
- nanotechnology

- coating
- shelf
- add

- metal

Nanorobotics Laboratory

Mr. Franklin introduced Jason and Duke to the other scientists at his laboratory.

Jason held Duke's leash in his left hand and shook their hands with his right.

One person gave Jason a white lab coat to wear so that he would look like a junior scientist.

"Does this lab coat have nanobots in it?" Jason asked his father.

"Yes, it does. The special nanotechnology keeps the white coat from getting dirty and stained."

They walked down a hall and stopped at a door with a
sign in big black letters.

The sign said, "Keep door closed."

"This is where I work."

Mr. Franklin opened the door to let Jason and Duke
inside and then closed it behind him.

Glass bottles sat on a table next to a microscope.

"Why do you have all these empty bottles?" Jason
asked.

"They aren't empty," Jason's father said.

"They are full of different types of nanobots."

Jason's father sat down in front of the microscope.

"Would you like to see what they look like?"

He turned on a big computer screen over the
microscope.

"Are there some under the microscope?"

Jason's father said, "Yes. So it's important to keep Duke
away from the table."

"Duke, sit." Jason held his palm out to Duke.

Duke sat.

"Good boy. Now lie down."

Duke lay down on the floor.

"Good boy. Now stay."

Jason took the leash off and set it on the table.

Duke blinked his eyes and put his head on his paws.

Jason watched nanobots crawling and turning around

and around on the screen.

- **turn on** (↔ turn off)
- **important**
- **keep away from**
- **hold one's palm out** (hold-held-held)
- **lie down** (lie-lay-lain)
- **blink one's eyes**
- **paw**
- **crawl**
- **turn around and around**

"They have tiny legs. They look like little insects," Jason said.

"These nanobots are tiny computers.

They kill cancer cells.

They grab the cells with their legs, and then they heat up the cells until they die." His father told him.

"Are nanobots just for doctors?" Jason asked his father.

"Oh, no. Nanobots can be in the soil to help farmers grow their crops.

Some fly high up in the sky to monitor the weather.

Others fly or crawl into small spaces to search for and rescue people in disasters."

"What else can nanobots do?" Jason asked again.

"Nanobots can be programmed to do just about anything we need a tiny computer to do." Mr. Franklin answered.

▲ Nanobots are helpful in farming.

▲ Nanobots rescue people in disaster.

Just then, a scientist opened the door and brought in a plate of warm oatmeal cookies.

"All of this work must be making my favorite junior scientist hungry. Would you like some cookies, Jason?" she asked.

"Yes, thank you."

Jason took the plate and set it on the table.

"May I look at more nanobots before I eat my snack?" Jason asked his father.

POP QUIZ

Fill in the blanks about the things nanobots can do.

ⓐ Nanobots kill __________ cells.

ⓑ Nanobots monitor the __________.

KEY WORDS

- insect
- cancer cell
- grab
- heat up
- soil
- **grow** (grow-grew-grown)
- crop
- **fly high up in the sky** (fly-flew-flown)
- monitor
- space
- search for
- rescue
- disaster
- what else
- program
- just about
- just then
- bring in
- a plate of
- oatmeal
- favorite
- Would you like ~?

Mr. Franklin put another slide in the microscope.

"Those nanobots have holes in them," Jason said.

"We call these nanocells," his father said.

"They are specially made to deliver medicine to cells in the body.

The nanocell goes inside another cell, and the medicine goes out through the holes."

Jason did not hear Duke quietly pad up to the table.

Duke put his paws on the plate and stole a cookie!

"Down, Duke!" Jason tried to stop Duke.

Duke's paw slipped.

He shoved the plate, and the plate bumped a bottle on the table.

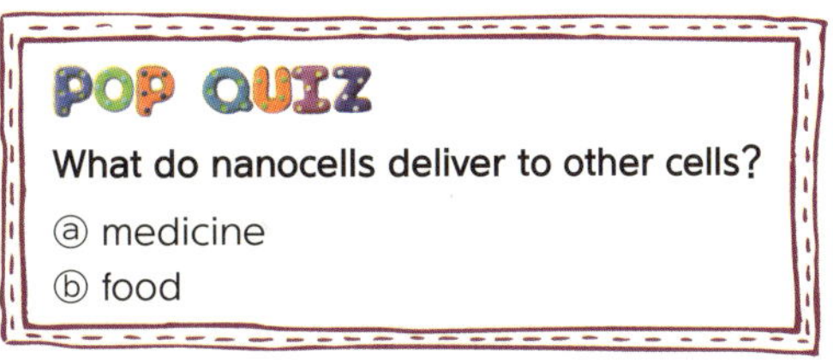

KEY WORDS

- slide
- nanocell
- deliver
- medicine

- go out through
- pad
- steal (steal-stole-stolen)
- try to

- slip
- shove
- bump

Down went the bottle! **Aha!**

It clattered to the floor, and the lid popped off.

Down went the cookie plate!

The cookies rolled onto the floor.

Duke raced to eat the cookie and ran through the mess to the open door.

The scientist who brought the cookies forgot to close the door when she left.

"No, Duke! Stop!"

Jason ran after Duke, but the Labrador was too fast.

Duke ran away down the hall with his tail held high.

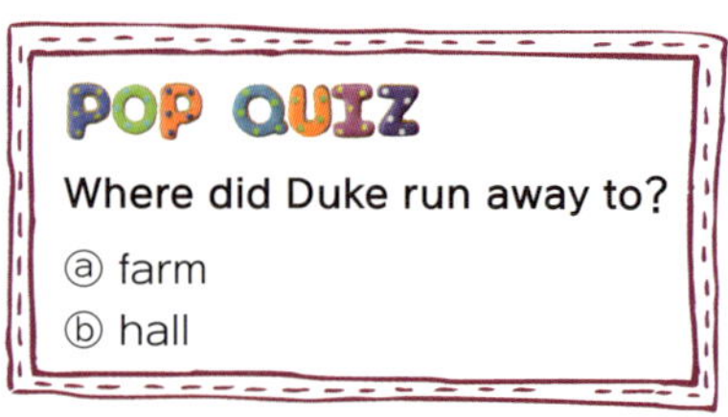

KEY WORDS

- go down
- clatter
- lid
- pop off

- roll onto
- race
- run through (run-ran-run)
- mess

- run after
- run away
- hold high

Keep door closed

Comprehension Quiz

A Fill in each blank with the right word(s) below.

> cookie plate clean stole looked like

❶ The nanotechnology kept the windows shiny and ____________.

❷ Jason set the ____________ on the table.

❸ Jason thought the nanobots ____________ little insects.

❹ Duke padded up to the table and ____________ a cookie.

B Put the sentences in order.

❶ The cookie plate went down.

❷ Duke quietly padded up to the table.

❸ Duke ran away down the hall.

❹ The cookie plate bumped a bottle on the table.

________ → ________ → ________ → ________

 Choose the best answer to each question.

❶ What did Jason wear in the laboratory?

a) special paper socks

b) a hairnet

c) a white lab coat

d) a medical shirt

❷ Why do nanocells have holes in them?

a) The holes let oxygen inside.

b) The holes let medicine out.

c) The holes make the nanocells weigh less.

d) The holes make the nanocells float in a person's bloodstream.

D Mark T for true or F for false.

❶ Jason heard Duke quietly pad up to the table. T F

❷ The scientist who brought the cookies left the door open. T F

❸ Glass bottles were sitting on the table next to the microscope. T F

❹ Sign on the door of Mr. Franklin's laboratory said, "Keep door open." T F

Chapter Three

Duke on the Run

Jason chased Duke out the door.

He saw Duke's tail go around the corner.

Jason ran around the corner.

Duke put his paws on the door of another laboratory
and pushed it open.

An alarm went off.

Ring! Beep! Ring! Beep! Ring! 

People ran out of their offices to see what had happened.

POP QUIZ

What did people in the laboratory do when
the alarm went off?

ⓐ They chased Duke.
ⓑ They ran out of their offices.

KEY WORDS

- on the run
- go around the corner
- push (↔ pull)
- go off
- run out of
- happen
- fall on (fall-fell-fallen)
- right now

Jason and Mr. Franklin ran into the room.

Duke bumped against a shelf.

Crash! Bottles fell on the floor.

Yelp! Duke jumped and shook his fur.

Whoosh!

He ran past Jason and out the door again.

"No, Duke!" Jason called.

"We can't play chase right now!"

Jason's father picked up a bottle from the floor and
frowned.

"Duke spilled smart dust all over his fur.

But that is a good thing.

We can track him on a tablet computer." 

Jason's father grabbed the tablet computer from the
desk, and they ran outside.

They saw Duke's tail wagging as he ran into a grove of
trees and disappeared.

Jason's father watched moving dots on the computer.

"He's going east."

"Let's go," Jason said.

They tracked Duke to the hospital one block east of the laboratory.

"I see him!"

Jason pointed to Duke sitting on the sidewalk in front of a person in a wheelchair. The person had unusual eyeglasses on.

▲ tablet computer

KEY WORDS

- pick up
- frown
- spill
- all over
- grove
- disappear
- dot
- go east
- block
- sidewalk
- wheelchair
- unusual (↔ usual)

The person blinked, and his wheelchair turned left.

Duke barked.

The person blinked again, and his wheelchair turned right.

Duke cocked his head and watched.

Jason's father laughed and said, "Duke is learning about nanobots that help people who are paralyzed."

"What does paralyzed mean?" Jason asked his father.

"It means the person cannot use his arms or legs.

But he can use his eyes.

When he signals with his eyes, nanobots in his special

glasses make his wheelchair move."

The person made his wheelchair move forward.

KEY WORDS

- cock
- paralyzed
- signal
- move forward

Duke followed the person and wagged his tail.

"He wants to play," Jason said.

"Here, Duke!"

Duke looked at Jason and wagged his tail harder.

Then, he yipped and ran through the sliding glass doors into the hospital lobby.

"Oh, no!" Mr. Franklin said.

"Dogs aren't allowed in the hospital." Aha!

Jason ran to the doors.

"We need to get Duke out of there before he gets into more trouble."

HOSPITAL

A List the places where Duke went in order.

❶ another laboratory room　　❷ hospital lobby

❸ a grove of trees　　❹ sidewalk

________ → ________ → ________ → ________

B Circle the right word for each underlined part.

❶ The person in a wheelchair had (unusual / ordinary) eyeglasses on.

❷ Duke moved to the hospital one block (west / east) of the laboratory.

❸ Duke spilled smart (dust / germ) all over his fur.

❹ Jason and Mr. Franklin can (rescue / track) Duke on a tablet computer.

C Choose the best answer to each question.

❶ How did Duke set off an alarm when he ran away?

a) He ran through a security field.

b) He opened a door of another laboratory room.

c) He bumped into a fire alarm button.

d) The security guard saw him and pressed an alarm.

❷ How did Jason and his father know that Duke ran to the hospital?

a) He looked out the window.

b) He saw Duke's tail.

c) He watched moving dots on a tablet computer screen.

d) He heard Duke barking.

D Mark T for true or F for false.

❶ Dogs aren't allowed in the hospital.   T F

❷ The man who are paralyzed made his wheelchair move with his voice.   T F

❸ Jason and his father saw Duke's paws in the grove of trees.   T F

❹ Duke was sitting on the sidewalk in front of a person in a wheelchair.   T F

Lost in the Crowd

Duke slipped into the elevator just before the shiny silver doors closed.

Jason was too late.

He watched as the elevator went to the third floor.

"What's on the third floor?" he asked his father.

"The third floor is the cancer treatment level.

This is where we bring the nanobots we develop for cancer detection.

If a person has cancer, the nanobots glow red.

Then, the doctors send in the nanocells that deliver the medicine."

KEY WORDS

- crowd
- silver
- treatment
- level
- develop
- detection
- have cancer
- glow
- knock over
- jars of
- go faster
- tap
- ping
- No dogs allowed!
- yell

"I hope Duke doesn't knock over any more jars of
nanobots in here."

Jason wished the elevator would go faster.

He tapped the button for the third floor again.

Finally, the elevator doors opened with a soft ping.

A nurse ran past them.

She was chasing Duke out of the room.

"No dogs allowed!" she yelled.

Another nurse picked up her phone.

"I'll call security."

"Please don't call security," Jason asked the nurse.

"Duke is my dog. I will get him and put him back on his leash."

"You'd better hurry," the nurse said.

"Your dog is running down the stairs now."

Jason and his father sprinted to the stairs.

A crowd of people walked up and down the stairs.

They were busy going here and there.

Duke disappeared into the crowd of people.

"Where did he go?"

Jason leaned over the stair railing to look.

A large woman got in Jason's way.

Her bag bumped him.

"Excuse me," she said.

"Will you please let me use the stair railing?"

Jason backed away.

KEY WORDS

- security
- had better
- hurry
- stair
- sprint
- a crowd of

- be busy *Verb*-ing
- here and there
- lean over
- railing
- back away

"I think we lost Duke." **Aha!**

Mr. Franklin put his finger on the computer.

"When Duke ran between the people on the stairs,
some of the smart dust rubbed off his fur and onto their
pants."

Jason groaned and put his hands on his head.

"Now how will we know where he is?"

"It is confusing because there is
smart dust all over the stairs
and on people's clothing."
Mr. Franklin said.

Jason waited and watched the computer.

It showed blue dots of smart dust swirling on the stairs
and going down the hall.

Jason had an idea.

"Can we switch to tracking Duke by his red dog collar?"

"That's a good idea!"

His father changed the computer setting.

In a minute, they saw a large blue dot moving fast.

"That's Duke," his father said.

"He's heading southwest toward the gold farm."

"What's a gold farm?" Jason asked.

"Our computers need gold to make them work. Our laboratories grow alfalfa on a farm behind our building." Mr. Franklin said.

"What does alfalfa have to do with gold?"

"Alfalfa takes gold from the soil. We have nanobots that go into the soil and get the gold from the roots of the alfalfa plants."

"Then do the nanobots bring the gold to the laboratory?"

"A gold farmer collects it with a special static electric mesh cloth. Then, we use the gold in our computers."

Through the hospital windows, Jason saw Duke romping in the field of green alfalfa.

"What are we waiting for? Let's go!"

▲ alfalfa

KEY WORDS

- alfalfa
- have to do with
- collect
- static
- electric
- mesh cloth
- through
- romp

Comprehension Quiz

A Circle the right word(s) for each underlined part.

❶ The doctors send in the nanocells that deliver the (<u>medicine /
blood</u>) into the body.

❷ Jason and his father tracked a large (<u>red / blue</u>) dot moving fast
on the tablet computer.

❸ Duke ran to (<u>southwest / northwest</u>) when he left the hospital.

❹ The farmer collects the gold with a (<u>magnetic metal detector /
static electric mesh cloth</u>).

B Mark T for true or F for false.

❶ Duke went to the second floor in the hospital. T F

❷ Duke was heading toward the gold farm. T F

❸ The nanobots go into the soil to get the gold from
the soybean. T F

❹ Gold is used in computers. T F

C **Choose the best answer to each question.**

❶ What action did Not Jason and Mr. Franklin take to catch Duke?

a) Jason and Mr. Franklin went to the cancer treatment level.

b) Mr. Franklin changed the computer setting.

c) Jason and Mr. Franklin sprinted to the stairs.

d) Jason called security.

❷ What happened when Duke ran into the crowd of people?

a) The people gave him treats.

b) Some people were angry at Duke.

c) The people chased him.

d) Some of the smart dust rubbed off Duke and onto the people.

❸ What do Jason and Mr. Franklin use to find Duke among so

many people?

a) security   b) smart dust

c) gold farm   d) another dog

❹ What plant is growing on the gold farm?

a) soybean   b) wheat

c) alfalfa   d) rice

Chapter Five

Down into the Dark

Jason and Mr. Franklin sped out of the hospital and turned left.

They ran down the street one block to the laboratory where Mr. Franklin worked.

They ran to the farm behind the laboratory.

"Where's Duke now?"

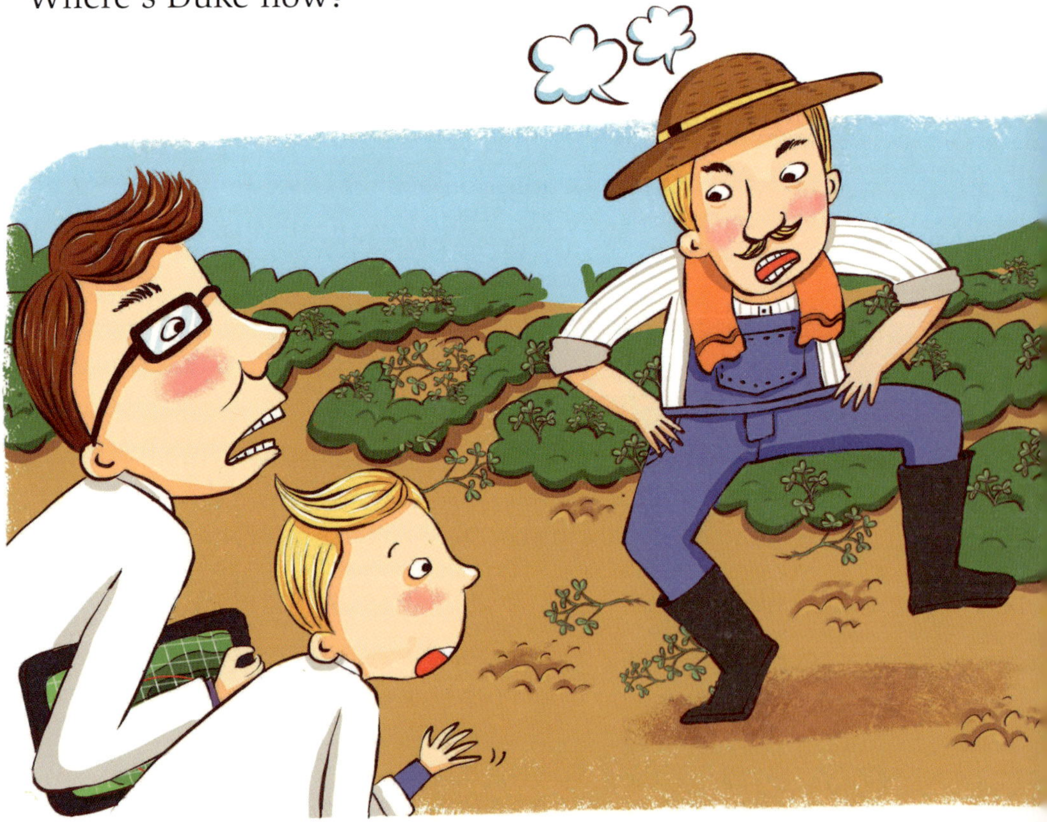

Jason searched the alfalfa field.

Duke had disappeared again.

An angry farmer walked up to them.

"Was that your dog?" he asked.

"Yes," Jason said.

"Do you know where he went?"

"He rolled in my alfalfa and made it flat.

Then, he dug a hole in my field."

The farmer frowned.

KEY WORDS

- **speed** (speed-sped-sped)
- **walk up to**
- **flat**
- **dig** (dig-dug-dug)

"I'm very sorry. Our dog is misbehaving.
We're trying to catch him and bring him back," Mr.
Franklin said.
"After he rolled in the alfalfa, he ran south."
The farmer pointed in the direction Duke had run.
Mr. Franklin checked the computer.
"It looks like Duke is thirsty.
He's heading toward an irrigation canal."
"That's where my nanobots monitor how much water I
use on my farm," the farmer said.
"They watch the water level and report it to me."
"They also keep track of the weather for you."
Mr. Franklin said.
The farmer nodded.
"Yes, if it's very hot, they tell my computer to let extra
water into the field."

KEY WORDS

- misbehave
- direction
- irrigation canal
- water level

- report
- keep track of
- nod
- extra

- take a rest (take-took-taken)
- Here, boy!

Jason looked at the computer screen.

"Right now, it looks as if Duke has stopped."

"He may be taking a rest after all that running," his father said.

"Let's go!" Jason said.

They ran to the irrigation canal.

They saw Duke lying down with his eyes closed.

"Duke! Here, boy!" Jason called.

Duke looked at Jason.

His ears perked up.

He wagged his tail.

Then, he ran away again!

"Duke is a bad dog," Jason's father grumbled.

Jason raced after Duke.

He saw Duke go into a restaurant next to the farm.

Jason went into the restaurant.

"No dogs allowed!" the cook told him.

"Sorry!" Jason said.

"I'll get him."

He grabbed a piece of bacon off a plate.

He followed Duke downstairs into the dark basement.

Jason's father turned on the light.

Duke hid behind a box in the corner.

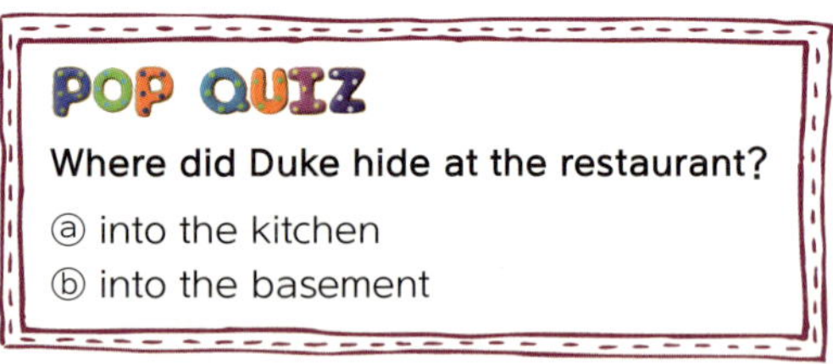

KEY WORDS

- perk up
- grumble
- cook
- downstairs
- basement
- light

"Here, Duke."

Jason whistled and held the bacon out toward Duke.

"I have a treat for you."

Duke poked his head out from behind the box.

He sniffed. He slunk over to Jason with his tail tucked between his legs.

"You've been a very bad dog," Jason told him.

"But I'm glad you're okay."

He held the piece of bacon on his hand.

Duke ate it and licked Jason's fingers.

Mr. Franklin snapped the leash onto Duke's red collar.

"At last! Now we are taking you home."

KEY WORDS

- whistle
- poke one's head out
- **slink** (slink-slunk-slunk)
- tucked
- lick

- snap
- at last
- whimper
- tremble
- growling

- tumble
- Cover your head!
- have an earthquake

Duke whimpered.

Just then, the ground trembled.

It made a growling noise.

Boxes tumbled from the shelves.

"Oh, no," Jason's father said.

"Cover your head! We're having an earthquake!"

▲ earthquake

Comprehension Quiz

A Who said what? Match each line with the right character.

❶   •   • a) "I have a treat for you."

❷   •   • b) "Cover your head!"

❸   •   • c) "He dug a hole in my field."

B Mark T for true or F for false.

❶ Duke rolled in the farmer's alfalfa and made it flat.   T F

❷ Duke stopped to take a rest at the irrigation canal.   T F

❸ Jason went into the restaurant to have a dinner.   T F

❹ In the basement, Duke hid behind a stair in the corner.   T F

 Choose the best answer to each question.

❶ What do the nanobots monitor in the alfalfa farm?

   a) How much alfalfa is in the field.

   b) How much water to give the alfalfa.

   c) How tall the alfalfa has grown.

   d) How much fertilizer to give the alfalfa.

❷ What did Mr. Franklin do when Duke licked Jason's fingers?

   a) He patted Duke on the head.

   b) He put Duke's leash on his collar.

   c) He made Duke sit.

   d) He took Duke outside the restaurant.

❸ What did Not happen in the basement when the earthquake occurred?

   a) The ground trembled.

   b) A growling noise was made.

   c) The big hole was made.

   d) Boxes tumbled from the shelves.

Chapter Six

Trapped!

"Quick! Get under this table!"

Jason huddled next to his father and held onto Duke.

The ground shook below them.

The building trembled above them.

Crack!

Wooden beams fell down around them.

The ceiling caved in, and a big piece of cement fell in front of the table.

A cloud of dust filled the room, and the lights went out.

They were trapped!

"Are you all right?"

Mr. Franklin felt Jason's arms and shoulders in the dark.

"Yes, I'm fine," Jason said.

"But I can't move my legs. Something is on them."

Jason's father grunted as he tried to lift the heavy beam off Jason's legs.

"It's too heavy. We need to get help."

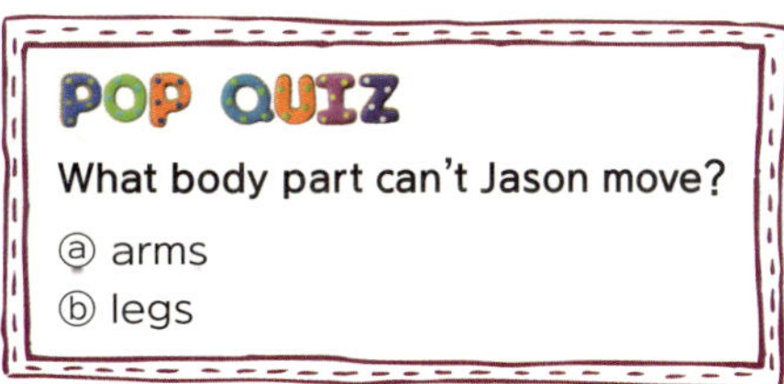

KEY WORDS

- trap
- huddle
- hold onto
- below
- above
- crack
- wooden
- beam
- fall down
- ceiling
- cave in
- cement
- go out
- grunt
- lift

"Help us! We're down in the basement!"

Jason's father cupped his hands and yelled toward the ceiling.

Jason yelled as loud as he could. Aha!

"Please, help!"

The dust choked him and he coughed.

Jason and his father yelled and called for help, but no one answered.

"The people upstairs probably ran out of the restaurant when the earthquake happened," Jason's father said.

POP QUIZ

What did Jason's father tie to Duke's dog collar?

ⓐ tablet computer

ⓑ nanobot

"Then they'll never hear us. How will anyone find us?"

Jason pushed on the cement. It would not budge.

Duke barked.

"Duke can get us help!" Jason said.

Jason's father typed on his tablet computer.

He tied the tablet to Duke's red collar with the leash.

"Are you ready to be a hero, Duke?"

Duke wagged his tail and licked Mr. Franklin's hand.

"Go, Duke," he said.

"Go to the laboratory and get help."

Duke squeezed out from under the table.

He climbed out of the basement and ran away.

KEY WORDS

- cup one's hands
- choke
- cough
- call for help

- upstairs (↔ downstairs)
- budge
- type
- tie

- hero
- squeeze out
- climb out of

"Are you still wearing your socks with smart dust in them?" Jason's father asked.

"Yes," Jason said.

"How will that help Duke?"

"The scientists in the laboratory can track us by the smart dust in your socks," Jason's father said.

"I put the setting in my computer just like I did with Duke's red collar."

"I hope Duke knows where to go," Jason said.

"I typed the laboratory address on the tablet," his father told him.

"If someone finds Duke, that person can take him to the laboratory."

"I hope Duke runs fast," Jason said.

They waited a long time.

The dust made Jason thirsty. Aha!

Finally, they heard voices above them.

"Jason, are you and your father in here?" a firefighter asked.

"Here we are!" Jason shouted.

He smiled when he heard Duke bark.

"This dog brought us the tablet that showed us where you are."

The person shined a flashlight into the dark basement.

"We brought some people to get you out of there."

Men with shovels and equipment moved everything out of the way.

They pulled Jason and his father out from under the table.

"I don't know how that table was strong enough to protect you," the firefighter said.

"It's an old table from my laboratory," Mr. Franklin told him.

KEY WORDS

- get out of
- shovel
- equipment
- out of the way
- protect

"We built it with special nanotechnology to make it stronger.

When we improved our laboratory tables, we sold this one to the restaurant to hold its heavy supplies."

"You're very lucky that table was in the basement."

"Yes, and we're lucky we brought Duke to work today."

Mr. Franklin patted Duke on the head.

"Duke, you and the nanobots saved the day."

Jason hugged Duke, and Duke licked his face.

"You are a good dog."

Duke barked and wagged his tail.

KEY WORDS

- **build** (build-built-built)
- **improve**
- **sell** (sell-sold-sold)

- **hold**
- **supplies**
- **lucky**

- **save the day**
- **hug**

A Mark T for true or F for false.

❶ After the earthquake, the lights went out in the basement. T F

❷ The restaurant sold the strong table to the laboratory. T F

❸ Thanks to nanobots and Duke, Jason and his father could save the day. T F

❹ Duke barked and cried at the very end of the story. T F

B Write the right answer to each question.

❶ Where did Jason, his father, and Duke go during the earthquake?

→ They were under a ______________.

❷ Who came to rescue Jason and his father?

→ The ______________ came into the basement.

❸ What made the table in the restaurant basement so strong?

→ Special ______________ made it stronger.

 Choose the best answer to each question.

❶ What fell in front of the table when the earthquake happened?

   a) a pile of boxes

   b) a shelf of dishes

   c) a chair from the restaurant

   d) a big piece of cement

❷ What did Mr. Franklin type into the tablet computer?

   a) the address of the restaurant

   b) the address of the laboratory

   c) the address of their home

   d) the address of the hospital

❸ How did the smart dust in Jason's socks help Jason and
Jason's father when they were trapped?

   a) The scientists in the laboratory could track them by the
      smart dust.

   b) The smart dust kept them warm.

   c) The smart dust sent out an alarm.

   d) The smart dust gave them some medicine.

Fill in the blanks to review the story.

❶ Title: __________ to the Rescue

❷ Main Characters:

Jason, Mr. __________, __________

❸ Sequence:

1. Jason asks to go to his father's n________ l__________.
   Jason gets a present of white __________, and Duke gets a present of a red __________ __________ with smart dust in them.
2. Duke steals a __________. He knocks over some glass __________ and runs away.
3. Duke runs to the hospital, and sees a person in a __________.
4. Duke runs to the gold farm and rolls in the __________.
5. Duke saves Jason and his father after the __________ when they are trapped in the restaurant __________.

❹ Details:

Nanobots
- are invisible to __________.
- kill __________ __________ and help farmers grow __________.
- monitor the __________ in the sky.
- search for and rescue people in __________.

Let's Think & Talk

Think about the following questions and answer them freely.

❶ Have you ever heard of nanobots? Tell us what you have learned about nanobots after reading the book.

❷ When nanotechnology becomes more advanced than today, how will our daily lives change? Tell us freely.

❸ In the story, Jason and his father said Duke was a good dog, and they said Duke was a bad dog. Why do you think they said he was both good and bad?

❹ If you were trapped in a basement like Jason, how would you do to escape?

Let's Review the Story

❶ **Title:** Nanobots to the Rescue

❷ **Main Characters:**

Jason, Mr. Franklin , Duke

❸ **Sequence:**

1. Jason asks to go to his father's nanorobotics laboratory.
   Jason gets a present of white socks , and Duke gets a
   present of a red dog collar with smart dust in
   them.

2. Duke steals a cookie . He knocks over some glass
   bottles and runs away.

3. Duke runs to the hospital, and sees a person in a wheelchair .

4. Duke runs to the gold farm and rolls in the alfalfa .

5. Duke saves Jason and his father after the earthquake when
   they are trapped in the restaurant basement .

❹ **Details:**

Nanobots
- are invisible to humans .
- kill cancer cells and help farmers grow crops .
- monitor the weather in the sky.
- search for and rescue people in disasters .

Smart Readers: **Wise** & **Wide**

After-reading Test

- Nanobots to the Rescue
- Level 3
- 28 Questions

(Vocabulary 7 / Reading Comprehension 16 /

Sentence Structure & Grammar 5)

1. Which of the following is similar to the word "track"?

   The scientists in the laboratory can <u>track</u> us.

   ① to follow and find   ② to be underground
   ③ to collapse or fall   ④ to call for help

2. Which of the following pair has the wrong past tense form of the listed verb?

   ① bring – brought   ② fly – flown
   ③ speed – sped   ④ slink – slunk

3. Which of these words means "tremble"?

   Just then, the ground <u>trembled</u>.

   ① monitored   ② shook
   ③ grumbled   ④ collected

4. Choose the right word for the blank.

   It was a ___________ of socks.

   ① plate   ② pair
   ③ grove   ④ jar

5. Which is NOT a pair of words that are opposites?

   ① show ↔ hide
   ② behave oneself ↔ misbehave
   ③ ordinary ↔ special
   ④ slip ↔ run after

※ Unscramble the letters inside each box to find the answer. And write the right answer to each question. (6~7)

6. What kind of a dog Duke is?

   → [rbaadrol]   (   )

7. What did Mr. Franklin add to the metal to make a stronger table?

   → [aoehooynntcnlg]   (   )

8. Looking at a calendar, what did Jason want to do on June 14?
   ① He wanted to eat dinner with his father.
   ② He wanted to show his father the school calendar.
   ③ He wanted to see his father's laboratory.
   ④ He wanted to circle his birthday on the calendar.

9. Why did Jason's father hesitate to let Duke come to the laboratory?
   ① There are expensive tools and machinery for nanobots.
   ② He believes the dog should stay in the backyard.
   ③ The dog might distract the other scientists.
   ④ The dog will be too tired to go to work.

10. Why did Jason work hard to train Duke to sit, stay, and walk on a leash?
   ① He wanted Duke to be in a dog show.
   ② He wanted to prove that Duke was a smart dog.
   ③ He didn't want Duke to get into trouble at the laboratory.
   ④ He wanted Duke to earn a treat.

11. Whom did Jason look like when he wore a white lab coat?
   ① a doctor   ② a junior scientist
   ③ his grandfather   ④ a farmer

12. What was sitting on the table next to the microscope in Mr. Franklin's laboratory?

    ① glass bottles

    ② glass microscope slides

    ③ a glass of juice

    ④ eyeglasses

13. What did Duke do when he saw the oatmeal cookie?

    ① He put his head on his paws.

    ② He barked and wagged his tail.

    ③ He sat and waited.

    ④ He put his paws on the plate and stole a cookie.

14. What is NOT true about Duke?

    ① Duke spilled smart dust all over his fur.

    ② Duke dug a hole in the gold farm.

    ③ Duke watched the water level near the irrigation canal.

    ④ Duke licked Jason's fingers.

15. Which was NOT mentioned that nanobots can do?

    ① They heat up the cancer cells until they die.

    ② They fly high up in the sky to monitor the weather.

    ③ They make people run fast.

    ④ They fly or crawl into small spaces to rescue people in disasters.

16. Which place did NOT Duke go after running away?

    ① hospital   ② gold farm

    ③ swimming pool   ④ basement in a restaurant

17. Which was NOT helpful for Jason and Mr. Franklin to be rescued?

① Duke

② tablet computer

③ nanobots

④ oatmeal cookie

18. Where did Jason, Mr. Franklin and Duke escape to when the earthquake hit?

① out of the basement

② under the table

③ near the shelf

④ behind the box

※ Choose the right phrase to complete the answer to each question. (19~20)

19.

> What did Jason grab off to catch Duke in the restaurant?
> → He grabbed ______________ off a plate.

① a slice of cheese

② a bottle of water

③ a cup of juice

④ a piece of bacon

20.

> What did Mr. Franklin tell Jason to do in the earthquake?
> → "______________________!"

① Close your eyes!

② Now lie down!

③ Cover your head!

④ No dogs allowed!

※ Choose the correct word or phrase for each blank. (21~23)

21. June 14 is ______________ a Child to Work Day.

① Working　　　　　　　　② Sleeping
③ Introducing　　　　　　④ Bring

22. The nanobots get gold from the ______________.

① alfalfa　　　　　　　　② soybean
③ bacon　　　　　　　　④ rice

23. The scientists in the laboratory can track Jason and his father by the ______________ in Jason's socks.

① tiny germ　　　　　　　② smart dust
③ nanocell　　　　　　　④ small insect

※ Choose the wrong part of the sentence. (24~25)

24. Dogs aren't allow in the hospital.
　　　　 ①　　②　③　　　④

25. Jason yelled as louder as he could.
　　　　 ①　　②　③　　　④

※ Choose the correct order of the given words to complete each sentence. (26~28)

26.
The dust __(Jason, made, thirsty)__ .

① Jason made thirsty   ② Jason thirsty made
③ made thirsty Jason   ④ made Jason thirsty

27.
I think __(lost, Duke, we)__ .

① we lost Duke   ② Duke lost we
③ we Duke lost   ④ Duke we lost

28.
The sign said, "__(door, keep, closed)__ ."

① Door keep closed   ② Keep door closed
③ Door closed keep   ④ Keep closed door

Memo

Memo

Suzanne Pitner

Suzanne Pitner is a teacher and writer who has enjoyed visiting Alaska, exploring Rome, teaching in China, and is looking forward to more world travel. She has a Master's Degree in Education, and is a graduate of the Long Ridge Writer's Group. In addition to writing educational articles and books, she writes historical fiction and contemporary fiction for young adults using the pen name Suzanne Lilly.

Nanobots to the Rescue

Written by Suzanne Pitner
Illustrated by Minjin Lee

First Published in February 2015

Editorial Manager: Juyon Choi
Editors: Jiyeong Park, Kyunghee Jang
Designers: Eunhee Lee, Elim
Cover Designer: Eunhee Lee

Published and distributed by

Darakwon Bldg., 64-1 Jandari-ro, Mapo-gu, Seoul, Korea 121-894
Tel: 82-2-736-2031(ext. 250)   Fax: 82-2-736-2037
Homepage: www.ihappyhouse.co.kr
Publisher: Kyudo Chung

ISBN: 978-89-6653-172-1 18740 / 978-89-6653-156-1 18740(set)

[Components]
- 1 Audio CD (Recording Studio: Aram)
- Answer Keys & Korean Translation: Free download at www.ihappyhouse.co.kr